EVERY DAY
WITH
JESUS

~

Devotional Collection

HINDS' FEET,
HIGH PLACES

Two Full Months of Daily Readings by
SELWYN HUGHES

BROADMAN
& HOLMAN
PUBLISHERS

Nashville, Tennessee

Broadman & Holman Publishers
Nashville, Tennessee
ISBN 0-8054-3088-1

Dewey Decimal Classification: 242.64
Subject Heading: DEVOTIONAL LITERATURE

Printed in the United States of America
2 3 4 07 06 05 04

Contents

INTRODUCTION

To see a wild deer springing from rock to rock, pressing ever higher into the mountains—gentle yet strong, graceful yet full of purpose—is to experience freedom in motion. Feet firmly on the ground, yet nearly flying. Stunning. Beautiful.

Would that we all were so fearless and alive!

Yet we can be! The secrets to spiritual freedom, of being able to tread the heights of God with power, grace, and agility, are found in His Word and freely available to all those who possess the courage to live them.

These principles call for bold honesty, for a transparency before God that clears the way for us to *really be* who we say we are. Such genuineness comes at a high cost—the cost of safety, of anonymity, of hiding behind hurts and fears and memories. But in the process of becoming real, we find ourselves shedding the weight of self-styled pretensions, loosening the bonds of human expectations, and stretching ourselves with the invigorating renewal of becoming the person God has made us to be.

Would you desire the sure-footed leap of the deer on the mountainside? Would you seek the high places at any cost to your personal pride and security? Would you walk with God in the freedom of purity, love, and truth?

Come . . . let us walk there together.

SPIRITUALLY SURE-FOOTED

"He makes my feet like hinds' feet, and sets me upon my high places." (18:33, NASB)

We begin a new theme that I hope will add greatly to your spiritual life—"Hinds' Feet on High Places." I read the story of a man who, while holidaying on a ranch in Wyoming, was given the use of one of its horses—the fastest he had ever ridden. One day a group of the ranch cowboys invited him to join them for a ride up into the mountains. As they climbed into the hills, they came to a dangerous ascent, at which point the foreman turned to the newcomer and said, "I think you would be well advised to take the longer but less dangerous trail to the top. Your horse is not dependable on the hills. Our horses are true climbers—their rear feet track exactly where their front feet are planted. Your horse has spent so many years on the plain that its rear feet could miss the track by inches, and one slip could mean serious injury—perhaps even death."

When I read those words, my thoughts turned immediately to the verse before us today, for no animal has such perfect correlation of its front and rear feet as the deer. When it leaps from rock to rock, its back feet land exactly where its front feet had been placed.

If we are to climb higher with God than we have ever gone before, then more is needed than just speed. We must know spiritual sure-footedness also. Let's determine we will let nothing stand in the way of making our feet like hinds' feet and climbing with God to the "high places."

PRAYER

My Father and my God, hear my prayer as I begin perhaps a new chapter in my spiritual experience. Help me to climb higher with You than I have ever gone before, and do it not only with speed, but with sure-footedness also. In Jesus' name. Amen.

FURTHER STUDY

Phil. 3:1-14; Isa. 54:2; Eph. 3:17-19
What was the deep desire of Paul's heart?
What did he pray for the Ephesians?

1. To press toward the goal to win the prize.
That Christ may dwell in their hearts.

CLIMBING HIGHER

*"He has made my feet like hinds' feet, and makes
me walk on my high places."* (3:19, NASB)

With today's devotional reading, we continue learning how
to become as sure-footed in the spiritual realm as a deer is in
the natural realm.

There are numerous references in Scripture where the pursuit
of God is likened to a deer climbing steadily, sure-footedly
toward the high mountain peaks—today's text being just one of
them—and the more we consider the simile, the more rich and
rewarding are the truths that flow out of it.

Why does God liken the pursuit of Himself to a deer making its way upward to the high places? And why does He focus
so much attention upon the deer's feet? Well, the deer has an
amazing ability, when climbing a steep mountain slope, of
ensuring that its back feet alight on the exact spot where its
front feet were positioned. This perfect correlation between its
front and back feet enables the deer to avoid the dangers that
would befall a less coordinated animal.

The Bible writers, in drawing attention to the sure-footedness of the deer, are attempting to show (so I believe) that what the deer experiences in the natural realm, we can experience in the spiritual realm. Do you really want to climb higher with God than you have ever gone before? Is there a deep longing in your heart to ascend, like the prophets and seers of old, into the mountain of the Lord? Then take heart—you can. This can be the greatest time of spiritual advance you have ever known. If you supply the willingness, then I promise you—God will supply the power.

PRAYER

O Father, my prayer is—make this the greatest time of my life. I long more than anything to ascend into the mountain peaks with You. I am willing—now send the power. In Jesus' name. Amen.

~

FURTHER STUDY

Isa. 55; Ps. 42:2; 63:1; 143:6

What did the psalmist express continually?

What does God promise?

My soul thirst for the Lord,
His word will not return
Void.

9

GOD HAS THE BIGGEST PART

*"He set my feet upon a rock and gave me
a firm place to stand." (40:2)*

The more we are acquainted with the way a deer functions in its natural habitat, the more clearly we can see the spiritual lessons that God wants us to learn. While the male deer, the hart, is a wonderful example of sure-footedness, still more wonderful is the female, the hind. Those who have watched it leading its young into the hidden fastnesses of the mountain peaks say it is the most perfect example of physical coordination that God ever made.

Why is this physical coordination so important?

When a deer moves upwards over a steep mountain slope, it proceeds by leaping from one spot to another. So it needs to be certain that its back feet will land on something solid. By positioning its front feet on something secure, it instinctively knows that if its rear feet land there also, it will proceed upwards in safety. If this were not so, and the deer's back feet were to land on a loose rock, then it would slip and meet with serious injury—perhaps even death. This sense of perfect coordination

10

is not something the deer learns; it is an instinctive ability given to it by its Creator.

And what God has done for the deer in the natural realm, He is able to do for us in the spiritual realm. Listen again to the words of the psalmist: "He makes my feet like hinds' feet." Note the word "makes." I find that deeply encouraging. It is not something I have to achieve on my own; He has a part in it too. And, may I add—the biggest part.

PRAYER

O Father, help me understand that although You have the biggest part in making my feet like hinds' feet, it cannot be accomplished unless I, too, do my part. Thus I willingly surrender to Your divine purposes. In Jesus' name I pray. Amen.

❧

FURTHER STUDY

Isa. 26:1-4; Ps. 92:15; 61:2; Matt. 7:24-29
What did Isaiah declare?
What was Jesus teaching?

The Lord is the Rock eternal
He is the Rock

TOGETHERNESS

*"Whoever says to this mountain, 'Be removed' . . .
and does not doubt . . . but believes . . .
will have whatever he says."* (11:23, NKJV)

Just as the deer's perfect correlation between its front and rear feet allows it to make its way swiftly and safely to the mountaintop, so the Christian who has a perfect coordination between the head and heart will rise to new heights with God. For you see, unless a person's head and heart are properly coordinated and move purposefully together, it is possible to miss one's step on the steep slopes of Christian experience and become a spiritual casualty.

I have known many Christians in my time who, because they lack coordination between what they ask for with their lips and what they want deep down in their hearts, stay in the same place spiritually year after year. They are not bad people; they just lack the spiritual coordination of the mature Christian, and thus they never know what it is to ascend into the mountain peaks with God.

Perhaps nowhere in Scripture is this truth more clearly portrayed than in the verse before us today. We are told that things happen in the spiritual realm when there is a perfect coordination between what we ask for and what we believe. When our mind and our heart are in alignment, when they track together with the sure-footedness of a mountain deer, then nothing shall be impossible to us. How many of us, I wonder, miss our step on the slopes of the Christian life because our hearts and minds are not properly and perfectly coordinated?

PRAYER

Gracious and loving Heavenly Father, slowly I am beginning to see the truth that underlies Your promise to make my feet like hinds' feet. Show me how to be as coordinated in the spiritual realm as the deer is in the natural realm. Amen.

❧

FURTHER STUDY

Isa. 58:1-11; Matt. 23

Why was the Lord displeased with Israel?

How did Jesus depict the Pharisees?

Calling them hypocrites

Because the appear to be

boasting on the out side only

NOT JUST WHAT YOU SAY

"Keep your heart with all diligence,
for out of it spring the issues of life." (4:23, NKJV)

I am convinced that one of the major reasons why so many of us fail to receive from God the things which we ought to be receiving lies in the fact that our hearts and our minds are not properly correlated.

Do you find yourself continually praying for things you never receive? I don't mean things about which there may be some doubt, but things you definitely know the Almighty longs to give you—love, joy, peace, wisdom, patience, the Holy Spirit, and so on. Maybe your mind is asking for one thing and your heart another. You see, it is possible to want something with the mind which is not supported by the heart. The mind is a much easier part of the personality to deal with than the heart, but, as our text for today states: "Keep your heart . . . for out of it spring the issues of life" (NKJV).

We can approach God with our minds and think that because we have a clear idea of what we want, God will give it to us, but the heart may contain hidden doubts which prevent

14

us from being fully integrated people. We fail to receive because we are not asking out of a fully integrated personality. As someone has put it: "God does not just answer *prayer*—He answers *you*." Those who wish to receive from God the things He delights to give ought always to remember that who we are is just as important (if not more so) than what we ask. God is not just listening to our words; He is listening to us.

PRAYER

O Father, the more I meditate on the need for heart and mind to be in perfect coordination, the more I am set on fire to become a fully integrated person. I know You are eagerly reaching down to me; help me to be as eager to reach up to You. Amen.

FURTHER STUDY

Matt. 15:1-20; Prov. 3:5; 23:7; Luke 8:45

What did Isaiah prophesy?

How did Jesus respond to Peter's request?

unwashed hands doesn't make a man unclean.

MISSING BY INCHES

*"You will seek me and find me
when you seek me with all your heart." (29:13)*

We are looking at what I consider one of the greatest truths we can discover about receiving from God: "God does not just answer prayer—He answers you."

The Almighty does not just listen to the words we weave into the air when we pray; He listens also to the attitude of our hearts. If the two are not properly correlated, then we miss out on many of God's blessings. And this missing out is not because God is stingy about the way He dispenses His blessings, but because we short-circuit our own spiritual system and become imperfect receivers. To put it another way: our failure to receive isn't due to the fact that God is not good at giving, but because we are not good at receiving. The fault is always in us, never in Him.

We are far enough along in our meditations, I believe, for me to ask you: are you a fully integrated person? When you present your requests to God, are your heart and mind as one? Is what you ask with your lips fully supported by what you are

16

saying in your heart? If not, then when you attempt to climb higher with God, you will not have the precise coordination you need in order to scale the precipitous heights. The awesome fact that has to be faced by all those who want to climb the mountains of God is this—it is possible to miss your step on those steep slopes not by feet, but merely by inches. And it is in those seemingly trivial inches that our spiritual direction is often determined.

PRAYER

O Father, I am seeing more and more the perils that come from being inwardly at cross-purposes. Help me, however, to see that although the challenge is great, the power behind me is greater than the challenge in front of me. In Jesus' name. Amen.

FURTHER STUDY

Joel 2:1-13; Deut. 6:5; Ps. 119:2
What was God's message through Joel?
When are we blessed?

A MISSED STEP

FOR READING AND MEDITATION—
PSALM 18:32-50

"You enlarged my path under me,
so my feet did not slip" (18:36; NKJV)

In my research into the ways of the mountain deer, I read an interesting but sad tale of a hunter who came across a deer grazing at the foot of a high mountain. He took aim with his rifle, but the bullet seemed to miss its mark. The startled animal raced towards the mountains, and the hunter watched in amazement as he saw it leap from rock to rock with consummate skill. Higher and higher went the animal, but suddenly its back feet appeared to slip, and although it struggled frantically to regain its footing, it fell hundreds of feet into a ravine and was instantly killed.

When the hunter arrived at the spot where the animal lay, he noticed a small burn on its flank caused by the bullet he had fired, which had simply grazed the animal without penetrating its flesh. The hunter says, "It was obvious what had happened. The graze had affected the deer's coordination, and in a moment when it needed to move swiftly and safely to the mountain height, it did not proceed with its usual perfect correlation. Its back feet did not land on the precise spot where its front feet had been, and although it was only an inch off, it was enough to bring about its fall."

This illustration must not be pushed too far and made to mean that a missed step on the mountain of God will bring about our own spiritual death. A missed step, however, will undoubtedly hinder our spiritual progress and prevent us from climbing as swiftly as we ought into the heights of God.

PRAYER

O Father, make me the kind of person whose heart and mind move forward into Your purposes with perfect unity and coordination. Help me not to miss my step— not even by inches. In Jesus' name I pray. Amen.

~

FURTHER STUDY

Ps. 40:1-5; Isa. 52:7; Eph. 6:15
What was the psalmist's testimony?
What are we to have on our feet?

Patient
Trust
Praise

On the Rock

INNER COHESION

"A house divided against itself will fall." (11:17)

One scriptural example that illustrates the need for a proper correlation between heart and mind is the Old Testament character, Amaziah. Second Chronicles 25:2 tells us: "He did what was right in the eyes of the LORD, but not wholeheartedly." His mind gave itself to doing right in the sight of the Lord, but his heart did not support his actions.

This lack of coordination proved to be his undoing: "When Amaziah returned from slaughtering the Edomites, he brought back the gods of the people of Seir . . . set them up as his own gods, bowed down to them and burned sacrifices to them" (25:14). Now look at how the life of Amaziah ends: "From the time that Amaziah turned away from following the LORD, they conspired against him . . . and . . . sent men after him to Lachish and killed him there" (25:27). Notice the steps:

(1) He was outwardly correct but inwardly uncoordinated.

(2) His inner disunity showed itself in outer disloyalty.

(3) This disunity resulted in his failure and death.

At the beginning, Amaziah does not appear to be a particularly bad individual—he just failed to be wholehearted in his commitment. He did all the right things outwardly, but his heart was not in them—hence, his spiritual ruin. We could say he missed his step by inches, but his fall was one of the worst ever recorded. If we are not held together by a single-minded devotion, our spiritual life can quickly go to pieces. Commitment to God demands cohesion—the cohesion of heart and mind.

PRAYER

O God my Father, help me to live a life of single purpose, with heart and mind moving together as one. Let me will the highest with all my being. In Jesus' name I ask this. Amen.

~

FURTHER STUDY

James 1:1-8; 4:8; Heb. 13:9
What makes us unstable? Not believing
What was the word of the Lord to the Hebrews?
Strength by grace.

ULTERIOR MOTIVES

FOR READING AND MEDITATION—
JAMES 4:1-12

"When you ask, you do not receive,
because you ask with wrong motives." (4:3)

There are many people in the Scriptures who appear to be spiritually minded but whose hearts harbor deeply unspiritual motives. Take the mother of the sons of Zebedee, for example, who according to Matthew 27:55 was one of the women who followed Jesus from Galilee in order to minister to Him.

Most commentators believe this small band of women to have been devotees of Christ, assisting Him and the disciples by preparing meals, washing and repairing clothes, and so on. Onlookers would have classified them as deeply spiritual, willing to give up their time to minister to Jesus—and of course, in the main, they were. In one place, however, the Scripture draws aside the veil from the heart of one of them, the mother of James and John, and shows her approaching Jesus with the request: "Grant that one of these two sons of mine may sit at your right and the other at your left in your kingdom." "You don't know what you are asking," Jesus said (Matt. 20:21-22).

Yes, she served Jesus. Of that there can be no doubt. But she had a secret and selfish motive in her heart: a privileged position for her sons. It is easy to excuse her action, as many have done, on the grounds that she was doing only what any other concerned mother would have done—attempting to get the best for her children. But Jesus saw right into her heart and said: "You don't know what you are asking." How sad that her beautiful ministry to Jesus was spoiled by ulterior motives.

PRAYER

My Father, help me to see that I cannot be a fully integrated person when I harbor within me two mutually exclusive loves. I cannot love You fully when I love my own interests fully. Set me free, dear Lord, to live only for You. Amen.

FURTHER STUDY

James 2; Eph. 2:3; 1 John 2:15-16
1. What motive was James exposing?
2. What did he say about the law?

HEART OF THE MATTER

*"Trust in the LORD with all your heart
and lean not on your own understanding." (3:5)*

What is the essential difference between the heart and mind? Many believe there is no difference and that they are really the same thing. But I see a clear difference between the heart and the mind: the mind is the part of us that thinks and reasons; the heart is the part of us that contains our deep longings and desires. Although the mind is important, the heart is even more important because it is the engine room of our personality— the part from which comes our drive and motivation. That is why our Lord says, "Out of the overflow of the heart, the mouth speaks" (Matthew 12:34).

Christ said that the words He spoke were the words given to Him by His Father (John 14:24). Does this mean the Father wrote out the words which He wanted Christ to say, and then Jesus had to learn them by heart? No—the heart of Jesus Christ was the very heart of God the Father; consequently, the words Christ spoke were the exact expression of God's thought. Jesus' tongue was always in its rightful place. He spoke not just from His head but from His heart; His heart and His mind were one.

Oswald Chambers put it like this: "The heart is the central altar and the mind the outer court. What we offer on the central altar will show itself in due course through the outer extremities of personality." In the search for unity of purpose and integration, there is no doubt that the heart of the matter is the matter of the heart.

PRAYER

O God, help me to be like Jesus, to pass on to others not just the things that come into my head, but the things that flow out of my heart. Bring my heart in closer contact with Your heart, dear Father. In Jesus' name I pray. Amen.

FURTHER STUDY

Mark 7:14-23; Prov. 4:23; Rom. 10:10

What comes from the heart? Evil

What was Jesus' teaching?

guard your heart

AN HONEST LOOK

*"Those with a noble and good heart . . . hear the word,
retain it, and by persevering produce a crop." (8:15)*

The first step in bringing about a more perfect coordination between heart and mind is *to take an honest, straightforward look at what is going on beneath the surface of your life.*

Over the years in which I have been writing the *Every Day with Jesus* devotional magazine, I have invited my readers from time to time to spend a few days taking an honest look at themselves. The reactions I have gotten to this suggestion have been quite interesting. Some Christians hear in my words a call to self-preoccupation and become concerned that I am pushing them toward becoming engrossed with their aches and pains.

One of my readers put it like this: "What people need is to forget about themselves and concentrate on reaching out to others; then their personal problems will quickly be forgotten." Others have taken an opposite position and said, "We need more of this, for our hearts are so self-deceived that unless we are constantly challenged in this way, we will never get through to a close relationship with God." I am unhappy about both those reactions, for both are unbalanced positions.

The first one fears that taking a look beneath the surface of our lives leads to unhealthy self-preoccupation. And the second opinion assumes that constant self-examination is the only way forward. But I believe an occasional, honest, straightforward look at what is going on beneath the surface of our lives contributes greatly to our spiritual progress, providing it is done in a proper and balanced way.

PRAYER

O God, help me to see that in inviting me to examine myself,
You are not seeking to demean me but to develop me; not to
take away from my spiritual stature but to add to it. Make me
an honest person—with You, with myself, with others. Amen.

FURTHER STUDY

Ps. 51:1-6; 15:1-2; Rom. 8:27

Where does God require truth?

What must we allow God to do?

of from your hearts

Search our hearts.

27

BELOW THE WATERLINE

"You desire truth in the inner parts." (51:6)

When considering the proposition that a balanced, honest look at what is going on beneath the surface of your life can contribute greatly to your spiritual health, think of your life as an iceberg.

We are told that the visible part of an iceberg—that is, the part we see above the water—is about one-tenth of its total size. Its bulk lies beneath the surface and is revealed only to those who are equipped to go down below the waterline. Our lives are like that; there is much more to them than we see on the surface.

Think of the visible part above the waterline as representing the things you do, the thoughts you consciously think, and the feelings you sense going on within you. Let the mass below the waterline represent the things that go on inside you that *cannot* be clearly seen or understood, such as motives, attitudes, impulses, and so on. Facing what goes on *above* the waterline—our visible behaviors and actions—is a whole lot easier than delving below the surface, and this is why many Christians (not all, of course) concern themselves only with what they can see, know, and understand.

These people can be described as "surface copers," who cope with life by dealing with whatever they can see and ignoring all the rest. If, however, we are to enjoy a deeper relationship with God, then we will do so only as we come to grips with the tough issues that lie beneath the surface of our lives.

PRAYER

God, help me this day to stand before You in complete and utter honesty. Save me from becoming a "surface coper," and give me the grace I need to face the things that I would normally avoid. In Jesus' name I pray. Amen.

～

FURTHER STUDY

Isa. 11; 1 Kings 3:1-10; John 5:30
How does Jesus judge and reprove? *with righteousness.*
What did Solomon ask for? *God a descerning heart to govern people and to know right from wrong.*

29

MORE THAN PERFORMANCE

FOR READING AND MEDITATION—
PROVERBS 23:12-28

"My son, give me your heart,
and let your eyes keep to my ways." (23:26)

Many Christians live on the surface of life and rarely, if ever, look below the waterline. They do have inner longings sometimes to climb higher with God, but their response to these feelings is to focus their attention on what goes on *above* the waterline—the area of performance and behavior. So they try harder in terms of more Bible reading, more prayer, more giving, more Christian activities.

I would be the last person to view greater obedience as unimportant, but it is not the only, or indeed the final answer. A great mistake made by many Christians who recognize they are not receiving from God the things they ought to be receiving is to think that the solution lies solely in more spiritual effort, the assumption being that as we do more *above* the waterline, the problems that lie *below* the waterline will all come right.

Now sometimes greater obedience and more responsible effort do have this result. I have often found, for example, that when a man who falls out of love with his wife chooses a change in behavior and deliberately sets out to do loving things for her, the loving behavior can trigger loving feelings.

There is more to spiritual change, however, than a change on the surface. It can *begin* there, but it is not complete until the focus moves from the surface down into the depths. Those who remain above the waterline in their Christian living and resist the invitation to look beneath the surface will soon become legalists—good at performing but bad at being.

PRAYER

My Father and my God, I see that if change is to take place in me, then it must take place in all of me. Help me to see even more clearly that while what I do is important, what I am in the depth of my being is even more important. In Jesus' name. Amen.

FURTHER STUDY

2 Tim. 3:1-5; Isa. 29:1-13

What did Paul say would be a characteristic of the last days? What was the Lord's complaint against the children of Israel?

"No Pretense"

*"You are like whitewashed tombs . . .
beautiful on the outside but on the inside
are full of dead men's bones." (23:27)*

The Pharisees of Jesus' day specialized in looking good. Sin was defined by them in terms of visible transgressions, and as long as they did nothing to violate the standards which they so carefully defined, they regarded themselves as being free from sin. And there can be little doubt about it—they were good performers. Their level of disciplined conformity to external expectations was very high. They impressed many by their performance, but there was someone they failed to impress—Jesus. He told them that they were nothing more than "whitewashed tombs" and called them "blind leaders of the blind" (Matt. 15:14, NKJV).

In His rebuke to the Pharisees, our Lord established a principle that must guide us in our effort to become the people He wants us to be, and that principle is this—there must be no pretense. Christ's teaching seems to be that we can't make it as His followers unless we are willing to take an honest and straightforward look at what is going on beneath the surface of our lives. To look honestly at those parts of our being which we would rather not know about is not, as some would have it, a sign of morbid introspection but a sign of healthy spirituality.

Always remember, our Lord reserved His harshest criticism for those who, like the Pharisees, made pretense and denial into a trademark.

PRAYER

O Father, You are boring deep—help me not to wriggle and squirm. Love me enough to overcome all my resistances, all my antipathies, and all my fears. For I don't just want to be a better person; I want to be a whole person. In Jesus' name. Amen.

FURTHER STUDY

Col. 2:1-20; Isa. 1:11-17; Gal. 4:10
What did Paul bring to the Colossians' attention?
How similar was it to Isaiah's word centuries before?

PRETENSE, CONSEQUENCE

"When Ananias heard this, he fell down and died. And great fear seized all who heard what had happened." (5:5)

Consider this story about a couple from the Bible who forfeited their lives because they pretended to be more spiritual than they really were.

Ananias and Sapphira were highly respected members of the early church and appeared on the surface to be deeply committed disciples of the Lord Jesus Christ. Doubtless, they had a fairly high degree of dedication, and they easily went along with the idea of selling their possessions and putting the proceeds into the treasury of the church. Their mistake, of course, was in pretending they had given their all when in reality they hadn't, and the consequences that fell to them because of their pretenses were swift and dramatic.

God deals harshly with dishonesty, but He is compassionate to those who see themselves as they really are, who confess this to Him, and who request His help in becoming the people they know He wants them to be.

I have known people who have stood up in front of a

Christian audience and talked about how wonderful it is to live a victorious Christian life, when in reality they were inwardly messed up. And I have known of others getting up before their brothers and sisters, confessing that though they love the Lord, they are experiencing great struggles and difficulties in seeking to live for Him. Who do you think is the closer to God? I will tell you—it is the one who is honest and open. Pretense repels God; openness and honesty draw Him quickly to our side.

PRAYER

Father, help me to be a sincere and transparent
person. Save me, I pray, from adopting an air of pretense
and masquerading as someone I am not. You delight in openness
and honesty. Help me to delight in them too. Amen.

FURTHER STUDY

Acts 19; Eph. 1; Rev. 2:1-5
Why did the word of the Lord spread rapidly in Ephesus?
What words did Christ bring to them some years later?

"OSTRICH CHRISTIANS"

FOR READING AND MEDITATION—
PROVERBS 20:15-30

"The spirit of a man is the lamp of the LORD, searching all the inner depths of his heart." (20:27, NKJV)

Most of us (myself included) are not good at observing ourselves and reflecting honestly on what goes on beneath the surface of our lives. Why is this so? I think one of the reasons is fear—fear of the unknown, fear of losing control, fear of spoiling a comfortable existence, or fear of having to face some unpleasant discoveries about ourselves. I have met many Christians in my time who adopt this attitude: however things are, good or bad, they could be worse, so it is better to leave well enough alone.

When we read the Bible, however, we discover texts like the one before us today, showing us that God has designed us with the ability to explore our deepest parts. We also hear men like the psalmist crying out to God: "Search me [thoroughly], O God, and know my heart! Try me, and know my thoughts! And see if there is any wicked or hurtful way in me, and lead me in the way everlasting" (Ps. 139:23-24, Amplified).

I want to stress once again that too much introspection is

unhealthy, but occasionally and in proper doses it is "good medicine." Those who resist this and pretend everything is well when it isn't are what a friend of mine calls "ostrich Christians." They have peace, but it is a peace built on unreality. When they lift their heads out of the sand, the peace they possess somehow falls to pieces. God's peace can keep our hearts and minds intact while we face whatever is true—outside and inside.

PRAYER

Father, save me from becoming an "ostrich Christian"—someone who pretends everything is well when it isn't. Nothing must be allowed to hinder the work that You want to do in my heart. Corner my soul and make me what You want me to be. Amen.

~

FURTHER STUDY

Mark 2:1-8; Matt. 12:25; Luke 6:8; John 2:25

How deeply did Jesus see into people's lives?

How deeply do you let Him penetrate into your life?

who they are thinking

WHY AN INSIDE LOOK?

FOR READING AND MEDITATION—
ISAIAH 33:10-24

*"This is the man who will dwell on the heights,
whose refuge will be the mountain fortress." (33:16)*

Before we can have feet like hinds' feet, we must be prepared
to take an honest look at what is going on beneath the surface
of our lives. Doing this, of course, can be dangerous unless it
is approached in the right attitude. Some Christians use the
process of self-examination as a means of avoiding rather than
assuming responsibility. They look at what is going on inside
themselves and allow what they discover there to develop into
a cynical negativism, which hinders rather than helps their
Christian life.

Those who do this fail to understand the purpose of godly
self-examination: to bring what is discovered to the Lord so
that He can deal with it. Many commentators have pointed out,
in the incident when the Israelites in the wilderness were bitten
by the snakes, that when they looked at themselves and recognized their condition, they were then highly motivated to look
to the brass serpent for help (see Num. 21:4-9).

The purpose of taking such an honest look at what is going

on beneath the surface of our lives is to promote a deeper dependence on the Lord and thus contribute to our spiritual effectiveness. Recognition of our true condition provides a strong motivation to look away from ourselves and turn in simple faith to the Lord Jesus Christ. As you take this journey into the core of your being, be willing to face yourself in a way that you have never done before. I cannot promise you it will be painless, but I can promise you it will be profitable.

PRAYER

Father, give me the courage to overcome the fears that would rise within me saying: "I am not sure that I can face it." Deepen the conviction within me that with You, I can face anything. Amen.

~

FURTHER STUDY

1 Cor. 11:23-33; Lam. 3:40; Gal. 6:4

How does Paul admonish us?

How does the writer of Lamentations put it?

examine y mc every and test than .

A Test of Honesty

". . . .He whose walk is blameless and who does what is righteous, who speaks the truth from his heart." (15:2)

We move now to the second step toward producing a perfect coordination between our head and our heart by facing this question: when I pray or seek the Lord, *is my heart fully and enthusiastically behind what I am asking for with my lips?* If not, we will fail to surmount the heights of God "with all four feet."

One of the things that used to puzzle me greatly in the early days of my pastoral ministry was to sit down with people who were not getting what they longed for spiritually and, after hours of counseling, sometimes to discover that although they were asking God for something with their lips, they were not really desiring it deep down in their hearts.

I am thinking specifically of a woman I knew who prayed earnestly (and loudly) in church for the conversion of her non-Christian husband. One day, however, in a moment of great openness and honesty (such as often occurs in counseling) she admitted that deep down in her heart, she didn't really want her husband to be converted because she was afraid that if he was, the attention and sympathy she was getting from people in the church would no longer be there. Once she realized what was going on inside her, however, she was able to deal with it and became one of the most spiritually released women I have ever known. Her whole life (not just her prayer life) became one of deep, quiet conviction, and eventually—many years later—she had the joy of seeing her husband surrender to Christ.

PRAYER

My Father, one thing is clear—such are the subterfuges
of the human heart that without Your light and guidance,
I can be self-deceived. Help me to apply the test of honesty
and openness to my own spiritual life. In Jesus' name. Amen.

FURTHER STUDY

Jer. 17:1-10; 23:24; 1 Cor. 3:20
How does Jeremiah describe the heart?
How does the Lord view the thoughts of the worldly wise?

"The Safety of the Old"

"Ask and it will be given to you; seek and you will find; knock and the door will be opened." (7:7)

In the illustration I used in the previous reading—of how a Christian woman with an unconverted husband came to see that what she was asking for with her lips was not what she was desiring in her heart—she finally had the joy of seeing her husband become a Christian.

But this must not be taken to mean that we have a guaranteed formula for bringing a non-Christian spouse to the Lord. It is right to pray with passion for those in our families who are not converted, but we must remember that each man or woman must personally surrender his or her will to Christ in order to be converted. People are admitted into the family of God only as they give up their commitment to independence and say, in effect: "Heavenly Father, I can do nothing to save myself; save me, in Jesus' name."

A man came to me complaining that he was not getting what he wanted spiritually. He told me that he had a deep sense of unworthiness, and although he prayed desperately for God to take it away, it stayed with him.

After many hours of talking, praying, and heart-searching, he came to see that although in his head he was asking for God to take it away, deep down in his heart he was not desiring it. He had lived with it for so long that he was afraid of the new positive feelings he would have to face if the negative feelings were not there. He preferred the safety of the old to the adventure of the new.

PRAYER

Father, day by day I am seeing more clearly the subtle devices of the human heart. Give me the insight I need to probe my own heart, to track down those things that may be preventing me from climbing into the heights with You. In Jesus' name I pray. Amen.

FURTHER STUDY

Luke 18:1-8; Deut. 4:29; Prov. 8:17
What characteristic did the woman display?
How can we be sure of finding God?

Clinging to Unforgiveness

*"Give me an undivided heart,
that I may fear your name." (86:11)*

A friend of mine who is a minister and Christian counselor shared with me about a woman who told him that she spent thirty to forty-five minutes every day asking God to take away from her an unforgiving spirit. She told Him that what she wanted more than anything in the world was the ability to forgive those in her family who had brought her hurt.

The minister joined her in prayer, but the Holy Spirit spoke to his heart and showed him that deep down, the woman did not want a forgiving spirit. The minister waited for the Spirit to show more, but nothing came. Realizing that he had enough information to pursue the matter, the minister invited the woman to explore the possibility that what she was asking for with her lips was not what she was asking for in her heart.

At first the woman seemed annoyed and upset by the suggestion that deep down she might not really want what she was asking for, but gradually she agreed to take an inside look. In the hour or two that followed, this came out—despite her claim that she wanted to forgive, deep down in her heart she clung to an unforgiving spirit. This gave her the justification she felt she needed when she was the cause of hurt to someone else. In other words, she was saying to herself: "Other people have hurt me, so it won't matter so much when I hurt them." When she saw what she was doing, however, she immediately surrendered it to God and found inner release and freedom.

PRAYER

God, I am deeply challenged by this, yet deeply relieved
to know that whatever might elude me can never elude You.
I open up my heart right now for inspection and examination.
Search me and make me whole. In Jesus' name. Amen.

~

FURTHER STUDY

Luke 17:1-5; Mark 11:25; Eph. 4:32   *increase*
How did the apostles respond to Christ's challenge?   *our*
How did Paul admonish the Ephesians?   *faith*

Be kind and forgiving

WHY MANY SLIP AND FAIL

FOR READING AND MEDITATION—
LUKE 11:1-11

"Forgive us our sins, for we also forgive everyone who sins against us." (11:4)

I drew your attention in the previous reading to the Christian woman who begged God to deliver her from an unforgiving spirit, yet deep down in her heart, she held onto it because of the way in which it served her unconscious purposes.

I want to suggest that you read the next sentence carefully, for in it lies the secret of the failure of many Christians to walk with "hinds' feet" to the high places which God has prepared for them.

If you harbor resentment or hatred toward just one individual in the world, by that much you are separated from God Himself.

By just that much do your rear feet fail to track with your front feet and, in the pursuit of God, you are in danger of slipping over the edge to spiritual failure. Let me put it even more clearly—if anyone has sinned against you and you have not forgiven them from the depths of your heart, then your attitude of unwillingness is a sin against God.

Listen to what the apostle John says about this: "If anyone

says, 'I love God,' yet hates his brother, he is a liar. For anyone who does not love his brother, whom he has seen, cannot love God, whom he has not seen" (I John 4:20).

The very first thing we must do if we are to climb higher with God is make sure there is no bitterness or resentment lingering in our hearts. If you have not done so before, turn now in thought to all those who have trespassed against you, and forgive them—fully and completely.

PRAYER

God, once again I plead for the insight and courage to see myself truly, for I may be cloaking my resentments with garments of piety. I would harbor no dangerous Trojan horses within me. Help me to be free of all resentment. In Jesus' name. Amen.

FURTHER STUDY

I John 4; 3:14-24; John 15:12
What was Christ's commandment?
Try memorizing I John 3:16 today.

FAMILIAR WITH FAILURE

FOR READING AND MEDITATION—
PSALM 145:1-21

*"The LORD is near to all who call on Him,
to all who call on Him in truth." (145:18)*

Many years ago, a young man came to see me and said: "I am not making a success of my life spiritually. I want with all my heart to become a successful Christian, but I seem to be failing in everything I do." At that time I was not as aware of the subtleties of the human heart as I am today, and I encouraged him to keep trying. I said, "Responsible effort and dogged obedience will bring you what you need; keep going no matter what." The advice I gave him was good, but it was not complete.

About a year later, after God had allowed me to see the subtleties and deceptions of my own heart, and after putting some personal things right before Him myself, I sat down once again with the young man and asked him how things were going. "A little better," he said, "but even though I keep asking God to help me become a successful Christian, I am still failing."

I took a deep breath and tentatively suggested that perhaps, deep down in his heart, he preferred failure to success. He looked at me in amazement and after a few seconds said, "Say some more about that. I feel you are touching something very vulnerable inside me."

We talked for hours, and he told me how all his life he had lived with failure, and it soon became obvious that he preferred the familiar feelings of failure to the unfamiliar feelings of success—even spiritual success. This one insight was all he needed to open up the whole of his being to God.

PRAYER

Father, if I too need something to trigger off a deeper openness and self-awareness in my heart, then give it to me today. I want nothing more than to be an honest person, not only on the surface but also at the depths. Help me—in Jesus' name. Amen.

FURTHER STUDY

Exod. 16:1-3; Num. 11:1-6; 13:17-33
What was the problem of the children of Israel?
Why were they not prepared to move forward?

THE DANGER OF DENIAL

*"Then you will know the truth,
and the truth will set you free." (8:32)*

It may be difficult for you to admit that perhaps your heart and your head are not spiritually coordinated. Many Christians are content to live above the waterline and insist that it is quite unnecessary to wrestle and struggle with the things that go on deep inside us. Their motto is: just trust, persevere, and obey. This is fine as far as it goes, but in my opinion it does not go far enough.

The effect of this teaching is to blunt the painful reality of what the Bible says about the condition of the human heart: "The heart is deceitful above all things, and desperately wicked; who can know it? I, the LORD, search the heart" (Jer. 17:9-10, NKJV). It is possible for even mature Christians to be self-deceived, to not really know their own hearts. This is why we must live in constant dependence on God, inviting Him from time to time, as did the psalmist, to "search me and know my heart" (Ps. 139:23).

There is a word to describe the attitude of those who ignore what may be going on deep inside them and concentrate only on what they can see above the waterline, and that word is—*denial*. In many Christian circles, maintaining a comfortable distance from what may be going on deep down inside is strongly encouraged. But nothing can be gained from denial. In fact, I would say it is one of the major reasons why our feet are not like "hinds' feet" and why we slip and slide on the slopes that lead upward to a deeper understanding and knowledge of God.

PRAYER

God, I realize I am dealing with something too devastating to pass over quickly or lightly. Help me be aware of the tendency that is in me to deny that I deny. Stay close to me at this moment, dear Father, for without You I can do nothing. Amen.

FURTHER STUDY

Gal. 6; Rom. 6:16-23
What was Paul's word to the Galatians?
How are we to walk?

THE CHOICE FACING US

FOR READING AND MEDITATION—
LUKE 16:1-13

"Unless you are honest in small matters,
you won't be in large ones." (16:10, TLB)

What is denial? It is the attitude that avoids looking realistically at issues and pretends that things are not the way they are.

Most Christians (myself included) are to varying degrees held together by denial. Deep down we sense that if we were to face the realities of life openly and honestly, we might not be able to cope, and so we pretend things are not what they are.

I know Christians who pretend that what they have in life satisfies more than it does, or pretend they haven't been hurt as badly as they have. They refuse to face and feel what is going on inside them, due to the strange belief that it is lack of faith on their part to admit to anything that is negative.

This faulty teaching—that we ought to ignore what is going on inside us instead of facing it and dealing with it—is responsible for more casualties in the Christian life than anything I know. A Christian psychologist says: "I am convinced that much of what we admire as spiritual maturity is a fragile adjustment to life based on the foundation of denial." I would agree. My own observation would lead me to say that I have found some non-Christians to be more open and honest in facing what is going on inside them than some Christians.

Is denial a wise plan for life? Absolutely not. The choice, then, is stark: either to deny and live comfortably, or to face every painful issue—and go on to climb the heights with God.

PRAYER

Father, help me to see that I need never be afraid to face anything, for in You I have the resources to resolve all problems, not just skirt them. Show me how to blast denial right out of my life—once and for all. In Jesus' name. Amen.

FURTHER STUDY

Eccl. 5:1-7; Isa. 29:13; Matt. 15:1-9
What do fools do?
What prophecy was fulfilled by the Pharisees?

A HEART PANTING FOR GOD

*As the deer pants for streams of water,
so my soul pants for you, O God." (42:1)*

The third step we must take if we are to be able to pursue God with a coordinated heart and mind is *to be willing to get in touch with the deep thirst for God which resides at the core of our being.* You will never pursue God "with all four feet" until you become intensely aware of this deep inner thirst.

The thought underlying the word picture in our text today is that of a deer craving for water during a prolonged drought or after having been chased. The psalmist said his heart panted for God, and the strong Hebrew word used here suggests a desire so intense that it is audible.

Do you pant after God in the way the psalmist described? Do you pursue Him in such a way that everything else in your life takes second place? I have to confess that I don't. Oh yes, I long after God. But I know I don't pant after Him in the way the psalmist described. And neither, I am convinced, do most other Christians.

Now don't react defensively and say: "Whatever does he

mean? My heart pants after God, and I will not let anyone try to tell me differently." Let me ask you to reserve any judgment you have on the statement I have just made, and I think I will be able to show you in some of the following readings that although you have a deep desire to know God, you still might not have gotten to the place where your heart pants after Him in the way the psalmist described. But take heart—you can.

PRAYER

God my Father, I would be rid of all that hinders my pursuit of You. Help me to see clearly into my heart, for I am so prone to defend myself. If there is something here that I need to know, then help me to look at it—openly and honestly. Amen.

FURTHER STUDY

Ps. 73:15-28; 27:4; 2 Chron. 15:15
What was the psalmist's confession?
What happened when Israel sought the Lord wholeheartedly?

"DO IT YOURSELF"

FOR READING AND MEDITATION—
DANIEL 5:13-28

"You did not honor the God who holds in his hand your life and all your ways." (5:23)

I said earlier that most Christians do not pant after God in the way the psalmist described in Psalm 42:1. Now I must attempt to make clear what I mean.

First, let me pull into focus the major problem with which we all struggle as soon as we are born. When God created us in the beginning, He designed us to have a relationship with Him. This means that deep within our being is a thirst for God which will not go away. It can be ignored, disguised, misunderstood, wrongly labeled, or submerged underneath a wealth of activity, but it will not disappear. And for good reason. We were designed to enjoy something better than this world can give us, particularly in the sphere of relationships. No human relationship can satisfy in the way that a relationship with God does.

This deep thirst for God that resides within us makes us dependent on God for satisfaction, and that is something our sinful human nature deeply resents. You see, due to Adam and Eve's sin in the Garden of Eden, we have all been left a legacy called "Do It Yourself." There is something within every single one of us that wants to take charge and have a hand in bringing about our own salvation. So here is the problem: to face the fact realistically that we inwardly thirst after God puts us in touch with a level of helplessness from which our sinful human nature shrinks. It reinforces the conviction that we are dependent on someone outside of ourselves for satisfaction. And that is something we don't care to acknowledge.

PRAYER

O Father, I recognize this elemental drive in my nature which causes me to resist standing in utter helplessness before You. But I sense that there can be no breakthrough in my life until I face this issue and deal with it. Help me, Father. In Jesus' name. Amen.

FURTHER STUDY

Ps. 143:1-6; 42:2; 63:1
What did the psalmist recognize?
What does it mean to "thirst"?

WRONG PLACES

FOR READING AND MEDITATION—
JEREMIAH 2:1-13

*"My people have committed two sins: they have
forsaken me, the spring of living water, and
have dug . . . broken cisterns." (2:13)*

The points I am making to support the statement from a
couple of readings ago—that very few people pant after God
in the way described in Psalm 42:1—must be followed with
great care. One of the major problems with which we are all
confronted is that we have at the core of our being a deep thirst
for God, which makes us entirely dependent on Him for satisfaction. Our sinful human nature resents this, because it dislikes
the feeling of helplessness that such dependence brings; it
prefers to have a hand in bringing about its own satisfaction.

This terrible tendency of the human heart to try to satisfy
its own thirst independently of God is brought out clearly in
the passage before us today. The prophet Jeremiah indicts the
people of God for depending on "broken cisterns" in their
efforts to quench their spiritual thirst—cisterns which they
themselves made but which can hold no water.

Note the two observations our text for today suggests: First, *the people were thirsty,* and second, *they moved in the wrong direction to satisfy their thirst.*

God said it was as if they walked right past the clear waters He provided and chose instead to dig their own well. They wanted to run their own lives and refused to come to God, allowing Him to quench their deep thirst. This stubborn commitment to independence is responsible more than anything else for preventing us having feet like "hinds' feet."

PRAYER

Gracious Father, I see that the problem You had with the nation of Israel is my problem, too. For far too often I try to dig my own well. You are searching deeply into my life. Help me not to evade or avoid any issue. In Jesus' name. Amen.

FURTHER STUDY

Judg. 17:1-6; 21:25; Prov. 28:26; 1 Cor. 10:12
How does the book of Judges sum up the human heart?
What was Paul's admonition to the Corinthians?

How Problems Occur

*"If anyone is thirsty, let him
come to me and drink."* (7:37)

We have put our finger on what, in my opinion, is the biggest single preventative to us having feet like "hinds' feet"—a stubborn commitment to independence. This reflects itself in the lives of every one of us—even those who have been on the Way for several decades. In the Garden of Eden, Adam and Eve, who were designed to experience fulfillment by being dependent on God, decided to act independently of Him. Sin can be summed up as a "Declaration of Independence"—an attempt to do for ourselves what only God can do for us.

What happened in the Garden of Eden is duplicated millions of times daily, not only in the lives of unbelievers but in the lives of Christians also—Christians who use self-centered strategies to satisfy the deep thirst that is in their heart for God. Almost every spiritual or psychological problem has at its roots this condition—the person is failing in some way to let God satisfy his deep inner thirst.

This might sound simplistic to some, but after many years of experience working in the field of counseling, I am convinced that this is what underlies such conditions as anorexia, sexual perversions, worry, hostility, depression, homosexuality, and so on. You see, if we are not conscious that God is meeting the deep thirst we have for Him on the inside of our being, then the inner emptiness will move us in one of two directions—to fill the emptiness in any way we can, or to withdraw and protect ourselves from the possibility of any further pain.

PRAYER

Father, I see yet again that until and unless my deep thirst for You is being quenched, I am in deep trouble and vulnerable to all kinds of problems. I simply must get this issue straightened out. Help me, dear Father. In Jesus' name. Amen.

FURTHER STUDY

Matt. 5:1-6; John 4:1-42
What was the message of Jesus to the woman?
How was this reinforced through the Sermon on the Mount?

THE PURPOSE OF LIVING

FOR READING AND MEDITATION—
LUKE 10:25-37

" 'Love the Lord your God . . .' and,
'Love your neighbor as yourself.' " (10:27)

The energy behind most of our behavior (particularly strange or abnormal behavior) is an independent attempt to satiate the deep longings which God—and God alone—can satisfy. If you want to know a biblical reason why people do the things they do, then keep these thoughts in mind.

A man said to me some time ago: "Why do I browbeat my wife and make demands on her which I know are not loving? And why, despite my best efforts to change, do I fall back into my usual patterns?" I told him: "Your legitimate longings for impact and respect are not being met by God, and as you can't function very well when these longings go unmet, you set about trying to get your wife to meet them." He saw the point, asked God to forgive him for drinking at the wrong well, and turned in a fresh way to Christ for life and power and reality.

But what about the person who goes in the other direction and withdraws from others, manifesting such symptoms as extreme shyness and some forms of depression? This person is someone who has little awareness of their thirst being quenched by God—hence a degree of inner emptiness—and is motivated to avoid moving toward involvement with others for fear he or she might be rejected.

Self-enhancement (a selfish attempt to quench our own thirst) or self-rejection—these are the two styles of relationship which characterize many Christians' lives. And both are a violation of the law of love.

PRAYER

Loving Lord, Your Word is crystal clear—the purpose of living is simply to love as I am loved. If I am not loving others, then quite simply I am not allowing You to love me. I am sinning in both directions. Help me, my Savior. Amen.

FURTHER STUDY

John 13:1–35; 15:12; Matt. 22:39; 1 Thess. 3:12
How do we show that we belong to Jesus?
What was Paul's desire for the Thessalonians?

"Easier to Pretend"

For reading and meditation—
John 5:24-40

"You refuse to come to me to have life." (5:40)

Why do most Christians not pant after God in the way described by the psalmist? Because to pant after God means we must get in touch with the deep thirst which is at the center of our being and acknowledge our basic helplessness—a feeling which our fallen human nature deeply dislikes.

Most of us instinctively draw back from dealing with this stubborn commitment to independence, pretending we are all right as we are. It is much easier to pretend we are thirsting after God than it is to face the challenge of giving up our commitment to independence.

I am conscious that the challenge I am putting before you is one I want to deny in my own life. There is something in me that would like to think—and would like *you* to think—that I have a heart that pants after God. But I know that if I stop short of identifying my independent strategies for finding life on my own and giving them up, I will never get in touch with the deep thirst for God that exists at the core of my being.

What is the answer? I must ask God to search my heart,

expose my self-centered motivations, and help me see just where it is that I stop short of panting after Him.

You see, the more deeply we sense our thirst, the more passionately we will pursue water. But we will never sense that thirst until we are willing to face the fact that we may be drinking more from our own self-constructed wells than from the wells of God.

PRAYER

Father, I tremble as I recognize this tendency within me to walk right past the fountain of living water and drink from a well of my own making. But help me to recognize it for what it really is—not just a terrible tendency, but a terrible sin. Amen.

FURTHER STUDY

Exod. 32:1-9; Isa. 28:12; 30:15; 2 Chron. 24:19
How did God describe the children of Israel?
What is said of them time and time again?

THE WORD THAT IRRITATES

FOR READING AND MEDITATION—
2 CHRONICLES 7:11-22

*"If my people . . . will humble themselves
and . . . turn from their wicked ways, then
I will . . . forgive their sin." (7:14)*

Most Christians never allow themselves to come too close to the deep thirst for God that exists at the core of their being, for if they did, they would be compelled to get in touch with their basic helplessness.

Why would we want to deny this? Because to recognize our helplessness puts us in a position where we have to repent of it—and that is something our fallen human nature pulls back from doing. Believe me, the one word which grates and irritates our carnal nature is the word *repent*. It is much easier to be given advice like: "Read more of the Bible every day," "Add extra minutes to your prayer time," or "Seize more opportunities to share your faith," than to be told to repent. All these things I have just mentioned may be excellent in themselves, but more is required if we are to get in touch with our deep thirst for God.

We must repent!

But repent of what? Our stubborn commitment to independence, as well as the awful desire and practice of choosing to dig our own wells.

A passionate pursuit of God demands this. Believe me, no matter what we say with our lips, we will never begin to pant after God until we repent of the self-sufficiency that has made its home deep within our hearts. This, in my opinion, is the biggest single step we can take in our pursuit of God and the experience of having feet like "hinds' feet."

PRAYER

Gracious and loving heavenly Father, help me to repent deeply. May I know at this moment a turning from self-dependence to God-dependence. I give You my willingness— now give me Your power. In Jesus' name I ask it. Amen.

FURTHER STUDY

Ps. 34:1-18; Joel 2:12; Luke 13:1-3

What was the central message of Jesus?

How does the psalmist express it?

"FAITH IN TWO MINDS"

*"If you have faith . . . you can say to this mountain,
'Go, throw yourself into the sea,' and it will." (21:21)*

The fourth step we must take if we are to have feet like
"hinds' feet" is *to learn how to face and handle any doubts that may
arise in our hearts.*

Most of us have to face the problem of doubt at some time
or another, and unless we have a clear understanding of what is
involved when we doubt and how to deal with it, our pursuit of
God can be greatly hindered. The English word *doubt* comes
from the Latin *dubitare,* which is rooted in an Aryan word
meaning "two." To *doubt* means to take two positions on something or to have a divided heart.

A major misconception concerning doubt—and one that
has brought great anxiety to many a Christian's heart—is to
view doubt as the opposite of faith, which clearly it is not.
Unbelief is the opposite of faith.

Os Guinness puts it like this: "To believe is to be 'in one
mind' about accepting something as true; to disbelieve is to be
'in one mind' about rejecting it. To doubt is to waver between

the two, to believe and disbelieve all at once, and so to be 'in two minds.' "

Donald Bridge, in his book *When Christians Doubt*, refers to doubt as "faith asking questions." Some might think this definition elevates doubt to a position it does not deserve and masks its true nature—but not so. It is only when we understand what doubt really is that we can deal with it in the way we should. Doubt is, as Guinness puts it, "faith in two minds."

PRAYER

My God and Father, I would be at my best—at Your best. But Your best cannot get across to me if doubt remains in my heart. Show me the steps I must take to overcome doubt. Amen.

FURTHER STUDY

Matt. 14:22-33; Luke 24:13-35
How does Peter illustrate being "in two minds"?
What did Jesus mean by "slow of heart"?

THE NATURE OF DOUBT

*"When they saw him, they worshiped him;
but some doubted."* (28:17)

A man whom I regarded as truly converted said to me: "I am riddled with so many doubts that I sometimes feel I am not a Christian at all." When I pointed out to him the nature of doubt—that it is not the same as unbelief—I saw a new expression appear on his face. He grasped me by the hands and said: "How can I ever sufficiently thank you? You have released a pressure that has been building up inside me for years."

I met him years later, and he told me that the simple insight I had given him concerning the nature of doubt was all he needed to face his doubts and deal with them in a spiritual way. I say again, no misunderstanding causes more anxiety to the heart of a Christian than that which concerns the nature of doubt.

Let's put unbelief under the microscope for a moment, for by doing so we will see the nature of doubt still more clearly. Unbelief is a willful refusal to believe, resulting in a deliberate decision to disobey. It is a state of mind which is closed against

God, an attitude of heart which disobeys God as much as it disbelieves the truth. It is the consequence of a settled choice.

Doubt is not a willful decision to disbelieve but a suspension between faith and unbelief. To believe is to be in one mind; to disbelieve is also to be in one mind, but to doubt is to be caught in the halfway stage between the two—suspended between the desire to affirm and the desire to negate.

PRAYER

Father, while I am relieved to discover that doubt is not the same as unbelief, I nevertheless long to live a doubt-free existence. Break down any barriers within me that would hinder the flow of faith. In Christ's name I ask it. Amen.

FURTHER STUDY

John 20:24-29; 11:16; 14:5; 21:2; Matt. 10:3
How did Thomas display his total commitment?
Why then did he doubt?

CORRECTING YOUR DOUBT

"Jesus reached out his hand and caught him. 'You of little faith,' he said, 'why did you doubt?'" (14:31)

While it is possible for us to distinguish between *doubt* and *unbelief* in theory, it is not so easy in practice. Doubt can move in the direction of unbelief and cross the borderline, but when it does, it ceases to be doubt. The idea of "total" or "complete" doubt is a contradiction in terms, for doubt that is total can no longer be classified as doubt; it is unbelief.

Os Guinness points out that when we attempt to undertake a biblical analysis of doubt, we can come out with either a "hard" or "soft" view of the subject. Those who take a "soft" view of doubt point to how vastly different doubt is from unbelief, and those who take a "hard" view of doubt point out its similarities.

Both views can be drawn out of the Scriptures. Error is usually truth out of balance, and it is important, therefore, that we get a balanced view of what the Bible has to say about doubt. In my view it can be summarized like this—doubt is not the same as unbelief, but unless corrected, doubt can naturally lead to unbelief.

This view has helped me avoid what I consider to be the extremes of being too hard or too soft on doubt. It is a condition which must be regarded as serious, but it need not be fatal. Don't allow your doubts to bring you into condemnation, for when faced and brought into clear perspective, they can be the catalyst to a deeper pursuit of God.

PRAYER

Father, when will I learn that in You all things serve—even doubt? Show me how to turn my doubts into stepping stones and use them to come into an even closer relationship with You. Amen.

FURTHER STUDY

Matt. 8:1-26; 6:30; 16:8
What phrase did Jesus often use?
What did He say of the centurion?

KEEPING OUR FAITH TRIM

"He is a liar and the father of lies." (8:44)

There are many things in life that at first glance appear to have no point. *Fear* is one such thing; *doubt* is another. I have heard it argued that all fear is of the devil and can serve no useful purpose in human life—but this is not true. Fear of being burned, for example, helps us avoid coming in contact with hot metals. Fear can have a positive purpose—and so can doubt.

Doubt, for one, can be used to help us detect error. We live in a world of which Satan is temporarily "prince," and he tries his utmost to get us to believe his lies. Jesus was not merely being poetic when He described Satan as the "father of lies." Half-truths and half-lies that masquerade as the whole truth are the devil's stock-in-trade. So because all things are not true, not everything should be believed. Some things clearly ought to be doubted.

One writer says: "The inescapable presence of doubt is a constant reminder of our responsibility to truth in a twilight world of truth and half-truth." It acts like a spur to challenge us to find out the truth about a situation. It is precisely because all is not certain that we have to make certain.

Francis Bacon put it like this: "If a man will begin with certainties, he shall end in doubts; but if he will be content to begin with doubts, he shall end in certainties." Doubt can act as a sparring partner both to truth and error; it keeps faith trim and assists us in shedding the paunchiness of false ideas.

PRAYER

Gracious and loving Father, thank You for reminding me yet again that I can take anything that comes and use it to positive ends—even doubt. Help me to use my doubts as a sparring partner to keep my faith trim. In Jesus' name I pray. Amen.

FURTHER STUDY

2 Pet. 2:1-10; Titus 1:9-11; 2 Tim. 4:1-5

What will come in the last days?

How did Paul exhort Timothy?

THE FIRST THING TO DO

FOR READING AND MEDITATION—
1 TIMOTHY 2:1-15

*"I want men everywhere to lift up holy hands
in prayer, without anger or disputing." (2:8)*

Although doubt can be turned destructively against error, it is also possible for it to be turned destructively against truth. How do we deal with the darker side of doubt? The first thing we must do is to bring every doubt into the open and examine it. Most Christians fail to do this; they do nothing with their doubts and just hope they will go away.

But the way people react to their doubts is an indication of their attitude to doubt itself. Many feel ashamed when they experience doubt and thus push it below the surface of their minds and refuse to recognize it. Some even regard doubt as the unpardonable sin. Others treat it as an unmentionable subject and never refer to any doubts they have for fear they are letting the team down. I myself sometimes struggle with doubt—even after more than fifty years in the Christian life.

In the months following my conversion, I had doubts about the inspiration and inerrancy of the Bible until I decided to accept it by faith. When I did, all my doubts concerning it were immediately dissolved, and from that day to this I have never had one doubt about the reliability of Scripture. But I have doubted other things—particularly in the area of personal guidance. I have learned, however, not to let doubts threaten or intimidate me, and when they come I simply look them in the face and say: "I am going to put you in harness and make you work to bring me closer to God."

Now my doubts get fewer and fewer.

PRAYER

Father, how can I sufficiently thank You for showing me how to take the negative things of life and turn them into positives? Nothing need work against me when I have You within. I am so thankful. Amen.

FURTHER STUDY

1 John 2:1-20; 3:24; 1 Cor. 13:12
What did Paul admit to?
What did John affirm?

TALK TO YOURSELF

"For the word of God is living and powerful . . . and is a discerner of the . . . intents of the heart." (4:12, NKJV)

Whatever we do, we must not let any lurking doubts go unchallenged. Pascal said: "Doubt is an unhappy state, but there is an indispensable duty to seek when we are in doubt, and thus anyone who doubts and does not seek is at once unhappy and in the wrong."

How do we go about resolving doubts? One way is to bring them to the Lord in prayer and ask Him to help us overcome them. If prayer does not dissolve them, apply the tactic which Nehemiah adopted: "But we prayed to our God and posted a guard" (Neh. 4:9). Take a verse of Scripture that is the opposite of your doubt and hold it in the center of your mind, repeating it to yourself many times throughout the day. Dr. Martin Lloyd-Jones once said: "Have you realized that most of your unhappiness in life is due to the fact that you are *listening* to yourself instead of *talking* to yourself? We must talk to ourselves instead of allowing ourselves to talk to us!"

In listening to our doubts instead of talking to them, we fall prey to the same temptation which caught Adam and Eve off guard in the Garden of Eden. The order of creation was stood on its head when the first human pair allowed themselves to be dictated to by the animal world (in the form of the serpent) when, in fact, they had been put in a position to dictate to it.

Don't let your doubts dictate to you. Turn the tables and dictate to them. Talk to them with words from the Word of God.

PRAYER

Father, help me never to be nonplussed, for in You there are ways to overcome every problem. Drive the truth I have learned today deeply into my spirit so that I may apply it whenever I am faced with doubt. In Jesus' name. Amen.

FURTHER STUDY

Gen. 3; Ps. 53:5; James 1:6
What was Satan's strategy?
What did Adam confess?

"THE DOUBTER'S PRAYER"

FOR READING AND MEDITATION—
JOHN 20:19-29

"Stop doubting and believe." (20:27)

If your doubts still persist after facing them, praying about them, and developing the habit of talking to yourself with a Scripture passage that refutes them, then seek the help of a minister or a Christian counselor. God has given us three resources to help us whenever we get into spiritual difficulties: the Word of God, the Spirit of God, and the people of God. The final answer to doubt may come as you share with an experienced Christian the things that are going on in your heart.

If you are not able to get the kind of help I am suggesting, then get in touch with your nearest Christian bookshop and ask them to recommend some helpful reading on the subject. Whatever you do, don't allow yourself to settle down into a complacent attitude about your doubts. Adopt a positive approach and determine to do something about resolving them. This will ensure that even though your doubts may take a certain amount of time to be cleared away, they will not be able to degenerate into unbelief.

Let me remind you of "The Doubter's Prayer" compiled by

Martin Luther:

> *Dear Lord, although I am sure of my position,*
> *I am unable to sustain it without Thee.*
> *Help me or I am lost.*

If the only thing you are able to do is pray, then that by itself will prevent doubt from becoming unbelief. If you also adopt the principle of "talking to yourself" from the Word of God, then you have in your hands the strategy for overcoming doubt.

PRAYER

Father, help me, whenever I don't know what to do, to turn naturally to prayer. Then no moment will be empty or fruitless. But help me also to utilize the power of Your Word, the Bible. Let these two things become my central strategy. Amen.

FURTHER STUDY

Mark 9:14-29; Matt. 9:29-30; 21:21

What was the father's request?

Do you need to pray that prayer today?

A DIP INTO THE DEPTHS

"Who may ascend the hill of the LORD? . . .
He who has clean hands and a pure heart." (24:3-4)

Once we agree to taking an honest and straightforward look at what is going on inside us, we must be ready for a number of strong spiritual challenges. But we must not allow ourselves to be disheartened, for we are soon coming to the end of what I consider the major conditions for moving upwards into the mountains of God.

The fifth suggestion I want to make to you is this—*recognize the subtle and insidious nature of sin.*

There is a view in the Christian church that as long as we focus on the sins that are obvious (sins of behavior), then we can forget any hidden sins that may be in the heart, trusting God to deal with them in His own way. Dealing with obvious sin is extremely important—don't hear me minimizing this fact. Moral discipline is part of the Christian commitment. We are expected to resist the temptations that come our way and correct any spiritual violations that may occur. But to concern ourselves only with obvious sin and avoid facing the sins of the heart will cause us to miss our footing on the slopes of God.

Someone has put it like this: "The grime has been so embedded in the carpet that a simple vacuuming will not do the job. We need a scrubbing brush and a strong detergent." Diligence in putting right the things that are obviously wrong is good, but without a clear understanding of how sin has penetrated our hearts, we will be nothing more than surface-copers.

PRAYER

Father, forgive me that I have been so content to live on the surface of life. Help me see that in turning my gaze to what is going on inside me, You are not seeking to demean me but to develop me. Give me grace not to shrink from the task. Amen.

FURTHER STUDY

Jer. 17:1-11; Gen. 3:8; Prov. 28:13
What is the tendency of the human heart?
What is one condition for us to prosper spiritually?

A LITTLE-KNOWN SIN

FOR READING AND MEDITATION—
PSALM 7:1-17

*"For the righteous God tests
the hearts and minds."* (7:9, *NKJV*)

Focusing only on correcting obvious sin (sins of behavior) without understanding what it means to deal with the issues of the heart will bring about a condition akin to that of the Pharisees—more smug than spiritual.

One of the things I have noticed about myself is that whenever I feel I am not pursuing God in the way I should, I tend to focus on the surface issues of my life—my above-the-waterline problems—and work at them all I can. But sin involves far more than what goes on above the surface; there is also something going on in the deep recesses of my heart.

As there is little need for me to discuss the sins that are obvious, I want to focus now on those that are not. I imagine that those of you who have been Christians for some time will expect me at this stage to identify the hidden sins of the heart under such categories as resentment, lukewarmness, impatience, jealousy, and so on. My concern, however, is with a category of sin that is not easily recognized and not very well-known. This sin is probably more deeply buried in our hearts than any other, and it acts, in my opinion, as a trigger to them.

The sin I refer to is—*demandingness.* You won't find the word in the Bible, but you will certainly see it illustrated there. Demandingness is insisting that our interests be served irrespective of others.

Clearly, if Christ is to live in us, then this has to die in us.

PRAYER

Father, I see that again You are about to face me with a strong and serious challenge. Forgive me if I draw back when Your lance plunges deep. I have lived with demandingness for so long that I might not even be able to recognize it. Help me, Lord. Amen.

FURTHER STUDY

Gal. 2:15-21; Isa. 29:15; 30:1-2; 1 Cor. 10:24
How did Paul describe "demandingness"?
What were the children of Israel doing?

THE EXAMPLE OF JACOB

FOR READING AND MEDITATION—
GENESIS 27:30-38 & 28:10-22

"If God will . . . watch over me . . . so that I return safely . . . then the LORD will be my God." (28:20-21)

One of the things we discover about ourselves when we look deep into our hearts is a spirit of demandingness. We demand that people treat us in the way we believe they should. We demand that people support us in times of trouble. We demand that no one comes close to hurting us in the way that we might have been hurt in childhood. Wedged tightly in the recesses of our heart is this ugly splinter which, if not removed, will produce a poison which will infect every part of our lives.

Let there be no mistaking this issue—if we are to pursue God wholeheartedly, then the spirit of demandingness which resides in every human heart must be identified and removed.

Jacob is probably one of the clearest biblical illustrations of a demanding spirit. He insisted on having his father's blessing for himself and took advantage of his brother's hunger, buying his birthright for a plate of stew. Later, Jacob went through a kind of half conversion, making God his God and giving Him a tenth and so on, but deep in his heart there was still residing this spirit of demandingness.

It shows itself again at Paddan Aram where, after marrying Rachel, he worked out a scheme to make himself rich at his father-in-law's expense (Gen. 30:41-43). He was still Jacob—the man who demanded to have his own way. He had talked about himself in terms of honesty—"my honesty will testify for me" (Gen. 30:33)—but it was nothing more than above-the-waterline honesty. His mind was changed, but not his heart.

PRAYER

O Father, I am so grateful that You have recorded in Scripture so many illustrations of the truths You want me to know. I see so much of myself in Jacob. Help me from this day forward to be less and less like him in this. In Jesus' name I pray. Amen.

FURTHER STUDY

Luke 15:11-32; Matt. 20:1-16
How did the prodigal's brother display demandingness?
How did Jesus illustrate it?

"WHAT IS YOUR NAME?"

FOR READING AND MEDITATION—
GENESIS 32:22-32

*"So Jacob was left alone, and a man
wrestled with him till daybreak." (32:24)*

The way in which God helped Jacob to be rid of his spirit of demandingness is revealing—"a man wrestled with him till daybreak." Like the Hound of Heaven, the love of God pursued him down the years, awaiting the hour when he would be ready to admit that he was beaten.

This man (probably an angelic representative) wrestled with him until Jacob's strength was diminished, at which point he asked him: "What is your name?" To us it seems a simple question, but in those days one's name was the expression of one's character; if the character changed, the name was changed. So Jacob, after a tremendous struggle, made the crucial confession: "My name is Jacob—the supplanter," he sobbed. The depths were uncovered. Jacob's heart was naked before God. The real problem was identified.

If you have not reached this place in your spiritual experience, I suggest you stop everything and tell God your name. You might have to confess: "My name is Demandingness; I insist on having my own way in everything." This may be hard to say, but get it out no matter what the cost, for there will be no new name until you say the old name.

The saying of the old name is a confession, a catharsis. When Jacob said his name, the angel said: "Your name will no longer be Jacob, but Israel" (v. 28)—a striver with God. The new nation of Israel would be named for this crooked man made straight. Jacob was buried; Israel was alive forevermore.

PRAYER

God, help me to tell You my name—my real name. Help me to dodge no longer: the game is up. Take out of me the spirit of demandingness. Change my name and change my character. Save me from myself. In Jesus' name I pray. Amen.

~

FURTHER STUDY

1 John 1:1-9; Ezra 10:11; 2 Sam. 12:13

What are we to do with our sin? *confess the*

How did Nathan respond to David?

The Lord have Taken away your sin,

DEMANDINGNESS IN ACTION

"We want you to know, O king, that we will not serve your gods or worship the image of gold." (3:18)

How does demandingness manifest itself? One way is by an insistence that God answer our prayers in the way we think He should. I talked with a woman whose husband had abandoned her and their three small children. As she talked, I grew uncomfortable, for she told me: "I know God is going to bring him back. If He doesn't, then He is not as faithful as He says He is. That can't be, so my husband will come back."

Can you hear the spirit of demandingness in these words? I sympathized with her hurt to such a degree that it was painful for me to have to explain this: that faith is one thing but demandingness is another. Her "faith" in God was based not on unconditional confidence in His character and sovereign purposes, but rather in the hope that He would relieve her suffering in the way she thought best.

Deep hurt is a most suitable environment in which we can wrongfully nourish a demanding spirit. Nothing convinces us more that God must answer our prayers in the way we think He should than when we are experiencing continued heartache. And the line between legitimate desiring and illegitimate demanding is a thin one which is easily crossed.

How can we be sure our desiring does not turn to demanding? When we are willing to say: "If God does not grant what I desire, then I can still go on, because I know that He will never abandon me, and in His love I have all the strength I need to handle whatever comes."

PRAYER

O God, save me from an insistent and demanding
spirit. You who are always reaching out to me in love and
awakening me, help me to recognize the difference between
a desire and a demand. In Jesus' name. Amen.

FURTHER STUDY

Matt. 26:36-46; Ps. 40:8; Eph. 6:6; Phil. 1:1
How did Jesus express desire without demandingness?
How did Paul express it?

FAITH, NOT DEMANDINGNESS

FOR READING AND MEDITATION—
HEBREWS 11:1-16

*"Now faith is the substance of things hoped for,
the evidence of things not seen." (11:1, NKJV)*

I am frequently asked: "Doesn't what you say about demandingness destroy the faith we ought to have when we approach God in prayer? Isn't powerful praying the ability to insist on God giving us the things we know we ought to be receiving?"

There is a world of difference between "praying in faith" and demandingness. When we "pray in faith," we have the assurance in our hearts that God wants to bring about a certain purpose for His own glory, whereupon faith reaches into heaven and pulls down the answer through fervent, believing prayer. Demandingness is another thing entirely—it insists on getting the answers that are in accord with its own desires rather than God's purposes. It is an attempt to bring God in line with our will rather than bringing our wills in line with His will.

Dr. Francis Schaeffer, when advised that he was suffering from a terminal illness, became assured that his work on earth was finished and that soon he would leave this world and go to his heavenly home. Thousands of people prayed for his healing, and when he himself was asked why he did not claim the Bible's promises concerning health and wholeness, he replied: "When I am in the presence of God, it seems uniquely unbecoming to demand anything."

Some have interpreted these words as a lack of faith, but I think I understand what he meant. It is one thing to plead and pray with passion for something very personal; it is another to demand that the will of the Almighty be one with our own.

PRAYER

Father, I see that the line between demandingness and faith is so fine that I can easily cross from one to the other without knowing it. Tune my spirit so that I will always be able to discern the difference between these two things. In Jesus' name. Amen.

FURTHER STUDY

Ps. 143:1-10; Matt. 12:50; James 4:1-15
What was the desire of the psalmist?
How does James put it?

THE ONLY CURE

"Take words with you and return to the LORD." (14:2)

How do we deal with demandingness? We must repent of it. Our passage today tells us how.

First: "Return to the LORD." The key to ridding ourselves of anything that is spiritually injurious is to return to God. The pursuit of God involves a shift away from dependence on one's own resources to dependence on God. Doing good and correcting wrong behavior does not automatically make us good people. Obedience is extremely important, but it must be accompanied by deep, heart repentance.

Second, the passage says: "Take words with you." This phrase means that we must put into words a clear description of what we are repenting of. If we are not clear about what is going on inside us, how can we repent of it?

Next: "Forgive all our sins." Repentance puts us in touch with God's forgiveness. We can work to bring about change also, but the greatest catalyst for change is humbly positioning ourselves before God and asking for His forgiveness.

Then: "Receive us graciously, that we may offer the fruit of our lips."

The thought here is: "Receive us that we may worship You more effectively." The purpose of all restoration is to worship God. We will be drawn into true worship when we give up insisting on our own way and learn to trust God for our own happiness. When repentance moves us from a spirit of demandingness to absolute trust in God, then we are in the place where God is able to make our feet like "hinds' feet" and equip us with the ability to ascend into the heights with Him.

PRAYER

Tender and skillful Invader of my heart, I yield my stricken being to You for healing. "Be of sin the double cure." Drain every drop of demandingness from my being. For I want not only to be better but to be whole. In Jesus' name. Amen.

FURTHER STUDY

Joel 2:12-18; Isa. 55:7; Ps. 34:18; 51:17
What does God not despise?
What does it mean to "rend your heart"?

"Too Good to Be True"

*"While they still did not believe it
because of joy . . . he asked them, 'Do you
have anything here to eat?' " (24:41)*

If we are to let nothing stand between us and the making of our feet into "hinds' feet," *we must understand the nature of disappointment and how it hinders our pursuit of God.*

All of us have been disappointed. Living in a fallen world means we have been subjected to experiences where we have been let down by others, even our loved ones at times. But this is not the problem—the problem occurs when we allow the hurts of the past to prevent us from reaching out to God and to others in an attitude of love.

A dramatic illustration of this is found in the passage before us today. It is the evening of the day of the Resurrection and, without warning, Jesus suddenly enters the room where His disciples are assembled and makes Himself known to them. How did they respond? "They were still unconvinced, still wondering, for it seemed too good to be true" (v. 41, NEB). It was obvious that the disappointment of Christ's crucifixion and death still reverberated within them. And now, faced with the reality of the resurrection, they did not want to believe it in case it were not true—and they would be disappointed again.

They wanted to believe, but they had difficulty in doing so because they knew they could not cope with what would happen in their hearts if it turned out to be untrue. Rather than take the risk of faith, they preferred—for a little while at least—to withdraw into the safety of disappointment.

PRAYER

God, forgive me that so often I allow the disappointments of life to deter me from moving toward You—in case something might happen that will disappoint me again. Help me to put everything I am and have in Your hands—with nothing held back. Amen.

❧

FURTHER STUDY

Luke 24:13-35; Job 30:26
How did the disciples express their disappointment? *with sadness*
How did Jesus deal with them?

"Surprised by Joy"

*"Weeping may remain for a night,
but rejoicing comes in the morning." (30:5)*

What a distinctive and intriguing difficulty it was for Jesus' disciples to struggle with disappointment, reluctant to believe in case what they were believing proved untrue. They were grown men whose lives had been far from sheltered and protected, yet the experience of the Crucifixion had been more harrowing than any of them ever cared to face again.

Over and over again during the days in which Jesus lay in the grave, they must have racked their brains to try to find some explanation for why His life had ended on a grisly cross. Doubtless, in the closing hours of that fateful weekend, their thoughts must have turned naturally toward how they might go about restructuring their lives. Then, suddenly, Jesus appeared to them. His appearance was everything they wanted, but such was the disappointment already in their hearts that they considered it too good to be true. Thus they adroitly protected themselves against the risk of being disappointed again.

This is the tragedy of disappointment—it can, unless looked

at and dealt with, reverberate inside us and hinder us in our pursuit of God. When disappointment is put into its proper perspective and when faith comes into its own, far from being too good to be true, one discovers that there is nothing else so good and nothing else so true. God proves Himself to be not just better than our worst fears, but better than our greatest dreams. No longer believing in joy is quickly followed by being surprised by joy.

PRAYER

Gracious and loving heavenly Father, give me insight into what I have been looking at today, and show me how to press through all disappointments in the knowledge that beyond the hurts, I shall be "surprised by joy." Amen.

FURTHER STUDY

John 21:1-22; Ps. 126:5; Isa. 35:10
How did Peter respond to his disappointment?
What were Jesus' words to him?

"IT'S OK TO FEEL IT"

FOR READING AND MEDITATION—
NEHEMIAH 1:1-11

"When I heard these things, I sat down and wept." (1:4)

Why is it necessary to know how to cope with disappointment? Because if it is allowed to reverberate in our hearts, however much we pretend with our minds that we do not care, our true feelings will prevent us from moving upward toward the peaks of God "with all four feet." Our back feet will not track where our front feet have been positioned, and thus we will miss our step on the steep slopes that lead us upward to closer fellowship with God.

The first thing we should learn about disappointment is this—it's OK to feel it. The worst possible thing we can do with any problem that arises in our lives is to refuse to face it and feel it. Yet this is a typical response made by many Christians to life's problems.

I once counseled a young, unmarried woman who had gone through some bitter disappointments both in her childhood and in her adolescent years. Such was the pain these disappointments brought that the only way she could cope with them was to turn her mind to something else. She toyed with the idea of drink, sensual pleasures, and several other things, but because she possessed a deep commitment to Christ, she decided to enroll in a Bible correspondence course. As we talked, it became clear to me that in doing this, her primary goal was not to learn more about Scripture but to relieve the pain of disappointment that was reverberating in her heart. Bible study became a way to escape from her problems rather than what it should have been—a way to confront them.

PRAYER

Father, help me to see that You have made me in such a way that I function best when I go through problems rather than around them. Show me that maturity means being in charge of my feelings, not my feelings being in charge of me. Amen.

FURTHER STUDY

Jonah 1-4; Prov. 16:32; Eccl. 7:9
Why was Jonah disappointed?
How did demandingness come into it?

COPING THROUGH CHRIST

"My soul is overwhelmed with sorrow to the point of death. Stay . . . keep watch with me." (26:38)

It is better to face disappointment and feel it than to pretend it is not there. And when I say "feel it"—I mean exactly that. Most people, I find, just walk around the edges of their disappointment, in the way they would walk cautiously around the rim of a volcano, admitting they have been disappointed but working hard (often unconsciously) to blunt the feelings of disappointment with a "let's not stay here too long" attitude.

The usual response to what I am now saying is: "Surely there is no point in being willing to enter into all the pain of our disappointments. What is past is past; isn't it better to forget the hurts and disappointments of the past and get on with life?"

Sounds quite rational and sensible, doesn't it? However, it is not the best way to deal with life. The more deeply we are willing to face our disappointments, the readier we will be to turn to Christ and draw from Him the strength we need to cope with them.

The danger we face when we are unwilling to feel as openly

as possible the disappointments that come our way is that we will come to depend on our own strategies to cope with them and turn only partially to Christ for succor and strength. Facing and feeling disappointment is a sure way of coming to recognize that God, and God alone, is the only one who can help us cope. When we face and feel our disappointments, we will cling more closely to Christ.

PRAYER

Gracious and loving heavenly Father, I want to live fully and frankly. Help me to face whatever goes on inside me with complete honesty. Save me from all self-deception and subterfuges, for I would be a fit instrument for You. In Jesus' name. Amen.

FURTHER STUDY

1 Kings 19; Heb. 4:15
What was Elijah's disappointment?
How did he respond to it?

SELF-PROTECTION

"And this is his command: to believe in the name of his Son, Jesus Christ, and to love one another." (3:23)

Another advantage of being willing to feel disappointment is that it enables us to come in touch with another hidden sin of the heart—self-protection.

Whenever we are disappointed, we naturally feel hurt and experience inner pain. Some people are so affected by this that a pool of pain builds up inside them, and they say to themselves: "People are a source of hurt. Stay away from them and don't get too closely involved." They see noninvolvement as the best way to avoid the pain of possible disappointment.

But this attitude is a violation of the law of love. Lawrence Crabb, a Christian psychologist, says: "Deficient love is always central to our problems." Behind most of our problems is a failure to love others as we love ourselves. If we refuse to move towards someone in the spirit of love for fear they may disappoint us, then we are more interested in protecting ourselves from pain than we are in loving—and that is sin.

Did you ever think of self-protection as a sin? Well, it is, and in my estimation it is one of the most subtle of all. Many of our relationships are ruined by this—particularly marriage relationships. A man who shouts angrily at his wife early in his marriage is setting up a self-protective system that says: "Disappoint me, and you will have to suffer the consequences." What is he doing? He is protecting himself more than he is loving his wife. And that, no matter how one might attempt to rationalize it, is sin.

PRAYER

Father, Your challenges are sometimes more than I can bear, yet I see the sense and wisdom that lies behind them. Reveal to me my own self-protective devices, and help me be willing to give them up in favor of loving as I have been loved. Amen.

FURTHER STUDY

Luke 10:25-37; Rom. 13:10; James 1:27
What did the priest and Levite display? disappointed
What did the Samaritan display? Love

ENTER AT YOUR OWN RISK

"Do nothing out of selfish ambition or vain conceit, but in humility consider others better than yourselves." (2:3)

Jesus is the supreme example of living without fear of being disappointed by others: He "made himself nothing, taking the very nature of a servant. . . . He humbled himself and became obedient to death—even death on a cross" (Phil. 2:7-8).

Disappointed people sometimes find it difficult to move out toward others. After all, people—even Christian people—can be rude, uncouth, obnoxious, and sometimes downright disgusting. I sometimes think it might be helpful if we put a sign outside some churches saying: "Enter here at your own risk." Forgive my cynicism, but I have lived long enough to know that Christians can hurt! What are we supposed to do when we know that to move toward another person in love exposes us to the risk of being disappointed? We move forward in love: easy to say, but more difficult to do. Making ourselves vulnerable to disappointment is frightening, but this has to happen if we are to love as we are loved.

Mature Christians are those who are willing to look fully

into the face of disappointment and feel it, knowing that because they do, they will come to a deeper awareness that no one can comfort the heart like Jesus Christ. In the presence of such pain, one more easily sees the uselessness of every attempt to find solace in one's own independent strategies. Facing and feeling the pain of disappointment underlies more than anything else the gripping truth that only in God can we trust.

PRAYER

Father, at times Your purposes seem to run diametrically opposite to my interests, but the more I ponder them, the more I see that You always have my highest interests at heart. Help me to trust You more—and myself less. In Jesus' name. Amen.

FURTHER STUDY

Matt. 26; 2 Tim. 2:13
What disappointments must Jesus have felt?
How often do you disappoint Him?

LOVE IS NOT BLIND

"Love never fails." (13:8)

If we draw back from facing and feeling our disappointments, then a part of us will experience spiritual deprivation. The more deeply we enter into our disappointment, then the more thoroughly we will see how committed we are to self-protection and turn from it in repentance to a more complete dependence on our Lord Jesus Christ.

Where have you been disappointed the most, I wonder? Most people to whom I address that question tell me: "My parents." It's surprising, though, how so many will not admit to being hurt or disappointed by their parents for fear they are failing to honor them or are being disloyal to them. Listen to what one writer has to say about this: "When someone appreciates his parents only because he overlooks the pain they caused him, his appreciation is not only superficial, it is self-protective. Love is never blind to others' faults. It sees them clearly and is not threatened. It admits disappointment but forgives and continues to be warmly involved."

Sadly, for far too many of us, love is not the bottom line—

self-protection is. When we can look into the face of every disappointment and be willing to feel the pain it brings, there is no more powerful way of motivating our hearts to turn in full dependence toward the Lord. If we are unwilling to do this, then we might cling more to our own ways of handling disappointments than we do to His. And if we do, then in no way can we climb to higher and more distant spiritual peaks "with all four feet."

PRAYER

Father, the more I become aware of what is involved in climbing higher with You, the easier it is to become discouraged. I am a dull, blundering disciple. Help me, dear Lord. Your grace works miracles. Work one in me today. In Jesus' name. Amen.

～

FURTHER STUDY

2 Cor. 12:6–10; Phil. 4:11; Eph. 3:16

What could have been a great disappointment to Paul?

Not having God's glory

What attitude did he take instead?

To be content

DELIVERANCE FROM FEAR

"Be strong and courageous. . . .
Do not be afraid or discouraged, for the
LORD God, my God, is with you." (28:20)

The seventh and last step we must take if we are to have feet like "hinds' feet" is to *ask God to rid our hearts of all and every fear.* I am convinced that perhaps millions of Christians are held back from pursuing God by fear.

Not all fears are harmful. When fear is spelled with a small "f," it can have useful, biological ends. It makes the frightened deer alert and fleet of foot; it makes the surgeon skillful, for he sees the dangers that beset him if he does the wrong thing. Fear harnessed to constructive ends may be constructive. When we use fear and control it, then it is good.

But when fear uses and controls us, it is bad. When fear becomes Fear with a capital "F," it becomes fearsome. I am sure that you have known times, as I have, when God beckons to you, as He did with John in the Revelation, to "come up here" (Rev. 4:1), only to find that as your mind got ready to begin the journey, your heart suddenly became gripped with fear. You wanted to move upward, but your progress was halted because you could not mount "with all four feet."

Overcoming fear ought to be one of our greatest objectives. The first spoken word of the Gospel was the voice of the angel: "Do not be afraid" (Luke 1:30). The first word of Jesus after His resurrection was: "Do not be afraid" (Matt. 28:10). Between that first word and the last, the constant endeavor of Jesus was to help us get rid of fear. We must learn His secret.

PRAYER

O God, give me deliverance from every harmful and
unproductive fear. I know this is a prayer that You delight
to answer, for You have fashioned me for faith, not for fear.
Help me, then, to surrender to what I am made for. Amen.

FURTHER STUDY

Matt. 14:22-33; 17:1-8
What caused Peter to sink?
What did Jesus say to the disciples on the mountain?

FEAR AND COLD FEET

FOR READING AND MEDITATION—
2 TIMOTHY 1:1-12

"For God has not given us a spirit of fear, but of power and of love and of a sound mind." (1:7, NKJV)

When Simon Peter stepped out of the boat and attempted to walk on the water to Jesus: "He was frightened, and . . . began to sink" (Matt. 14:30, Amplified). Fear makes you sink.

When Jesus healed the paralytic, His first word was: "Take heart, son," and His second: "Your sins are forgiven" (Matt. 9:2). When Jesus lifted the guilt, this lifted the fear which, in turn, lifted the paralysis.

When the disciples fell on their faces at the top of the Mount of Transfiguration, terrified because they had heard the voice of God, Jesus said: "Rise, and have no fear" (Matt. 17:7, RSV). Fear puts you down; faith lifts you up.

The man who brought back the unused talent said: "I was afraid and went out and hid your talent" (Matt. 25:25). His life investment was in a hole in the ground! Fear did it.

Again, it was said of the disciples that they were gathered "with the doors locked for fear of the Jews" (John 20:19). Fear always puts you behind closed doors; it causes you to become an ingrown person.

Joseph of Arimathea was "a disciple of Jesus, but secretly because he feared the Jews" (John 19:38). Fear always drives a person underground.

A man I know says that fear gave him cold feet. Prior to the Lord delivering him from fear, his circulation was so bad that he had to wear socks in bed. "Now," he says, "my circulation is normal. God took away my fear and gave me warm feet."

PRAYER

God, I see that fear is indeed costly. It is so costly that I dare not keep it. But I cannot easily get rid of it, for it has put its roots deep within me. Help me tear it up, root and branch. In Jesus' name I pray. Amen.

~

FURTHER STUDY

Mark 4:35-41; 5:25-34

What had Jesus said to His disciples? *Do you still have no faith*

What had this caused Him to do?

To lose His power.

HOMEGROWN FEARS

"He said to his disciples, 'Why are you so afraid?
Do you still have no faith?'" (4:40)

Some social scientists maintain that there are no inherent fears except two; the rest are acquired. The two inherent fears, they say, are the fear of falling and the fear of loud noises.

I read of some psychologists who examined five hundred people and found that, between them, they had about seven thousand fears. The theory that we inherit just two fears, of course, is not a proven fact, but if that happens to be so, then those five hundred people were loading themselves down with hundreds of unnatural and useless fears!

Once when I was in India, I was told of a caste where the women on each of their birthdays add four rings of heavy brass—one on each ankle and one on each arm. By the time they are in middle age, they walk with great difficulty under this senseless burden. But this is no more senseless than weighting oneself down with useless fears: fear of failure, fear of rejection, fear of the future, fear of growing old, fear of what people might think, and so on. Most of our fears are homegrown—

they come out of wrong home teaching and example. Parents who try to control their children by fear often succeed too well; their children grow up being controlled by the fears themselves.

A woman wrote to me and said: "All my life I have been a victim of fear. My nightly prayer was: 'Lord, thank You for not letting anything too bad happen to me today.' You said if I turned to Christ, He would rid me of all fear. Well, I have—and He did."

PRAYER

Father, we have filled Your world and our hearts with fear—needless, devastating fears. Help us, we pray, to find release from these fears, for they are not our real selves— they are an importation. In Jesus' name I pray. Amen.

FURTHER STUDY

Ps. 34:1-22; 23:4; Prov. 9:10; 19:23
What was David's testimony?
How can we find freedom from our fears?

TWO BASIC FEARS

*". . . and free those who all their lives were
held in slavery by their fear of death." (2:15)*

Psychologists are at pains to point out that fear is different from anxiety. Fear has a specific object, whereas anxiety is a vague and unspecified apprehension.

What, I wonder, is your biggest fear? Benjamin Rank, a social scientist, says that there are basically two forms of fear: the fear of life and the fear of death. The fear of life is the fear of having to live as an isolated individual. The fear of death is the fear of losing individuality. He says: "Between these two fear possibilities, these poles of fear, the individual is thrown back and forth all his life."

The first fear—the fear of life—is vividly illustrated by a small boy's comment: "I suppose the reason for twins is because little children don't like to come into the world alone." The fear of life makes many retreat into illness. It is a refuge from responsibility. Freud found the cause of neurosis in the past—in childhood; Jung, a disciple of Freud, found it in the present. He said: "I ask, what is the necessary task which the patient will not accomplish?" Backing out of life's responsibilities through fear of life is a major cause of problems.

But with many, it is the fear of death that paralyzes them. Our verse today reads, in speaking of Jesus, that He is able to "liberate those who, through fear of death, had all their lifetime been in servitude" (Heb. 2:15, NEB). Is it necessary to live under such servitude? Of course not. When Christ has all of you, then fear can have no part of you. It is as simple as that!

PRAYER

Father, I am so thankful that You have made it possible for me not to be enslaved by fear. I can be free, gloriously free—and free now. Touch me in the deepest parts of my being this day and set me free from all and every fear. In Jesus' name. Amen.

FURTHER STUDY

1 Cor. 15; 2 Cor. 5:1; John 11:25-26
What is the hope of every believer?
Is this your hope?

THE WAY OUT OF FEAR

FOR READING AND MEDITATION—
ROMANS 8:1-17

*"You did not receive a spirit that makes you a slave . . .
to fear, but you received the Spirit of sonship." (8:15)*

To be rid of fear:

First, if you have any fear, don't be afraid to admit it. To try to
conceal it is to reveal it in hurtful ways. Reveal it in a sound way,
and then you will not reveal it in hurtful ways. Bring all your
fears out into the open and look at them.

Second, give up all justification for your fears. Very often fear
produces bodily sicknesses that help us gain power over others.
We "enjoy" bad health. This possibility has to be faced before
you can ask God to deliver you from fear.

Third, to be controlled by fear is a fool's business, so stop being a fool.
One schoolteacher said: "I have been a teacher for thirty years,
but I always have nervous indigestion a week before school
begins." He was afraid of the children, and probably the children were also afraid of him. And neither had anything to fear
except fear. Am I being too hard in urging you not to be a fool?
Does this sound too cross an admonition? I'm only echoing my
Master, who said: "O foolish ones, and slow of heart to

believe" (Luke 24:25, NKJV).

Fourth, remember that every fear you face has been defeated by Jesus Christ. When any fear rises up within you, just calmly look it in the eye and say: "I am not afraid of you. You have been decisively beaten by my Lord. Bend your neck! There, I knew it. There is a footprint of the Son of God upon your neck." This confidence is your starting point. Nothing can touch you that hasn't touched Him and been defeated.

PRAYER

Father, help me never justify any unproductive fear, for when I do, I cut myself off from Your redemption. I can live without all fear when I live with You. Set me free—gloriously free. Amen.

FURTHER STUDY

Luke 4:1-19; Isa. 61:1; John 8:31-32; Rom. 8:2
What was Christ's mission?
Will you let Him minister to you in this way today?

STRONGER THAN FEAR

*"There is no fear in love. But
perfect love drives out fear." (4:18)*

In addition to the four steps out of fear outlined in the previous reading, let us consider two more.

Fifth, surrender all your fears into God's hands. This isn't as easy as it sounds, for it probably means the giving up of a whole life strategy. You may have been using your fears as a crutch; now I am asking you to renounce them. Can you do that? You can if you are willing to depend on Christ for your life rather than depending on your wits. You will be tempted to compromise—half give them up and half keep them in your hands. But this halfwayness will mean a whole failure. If you surrender your fears into God's hands, this means He now has them, not you. This shifts the basis: you are no longer struggling to overcome them; you and God are working it out together. To look at God creates faith; to look at yourself creates more fear—fear of fear.

Sixth, keep repeating to yourself the verse at the top of this page: "Perfect love drives out fear." If there is no fear in love, then the obvious thing to do is to love. Fear can only come where love is not. Where love is, fear is not. How do you love? Don't work it up. Just open your heart to the love that is in God's heart. Remember His Word that says: "We love because he first loved us" (I John 4:19). You will discover that as His love comes in, so fear will move out. Thus free of fear, your heart and mind will move in a coordinated fashion, fleet-footed up into the hills of God.

PRAYER

Father, now that all my fears are turned over to You, help me to open my heart to the great Niagara of Your love. Pour Your love into every corner of my heart until every one of my fears has been drowned. In Jesus' name. Amen.

FURTHER STUDY

Ps. 118:1-6; 3:6; 27:3; Isa. 12:2
What did the psalmist declare?
Why was Isaiah not afraid?

A FINAL SUMMARY

FOR READING AND MEDITATION—
ISAIAH 35:1-10

"Then will the lame leap like a deer." (35:6)

We have identified seven things necessary for a more perfect coordination between the heart and mind:

(1) Prepare to take an honest look at what is going on beneath the surface of your life.

(2) Face the question: When I pray, is my heart enthusiastically behind what I ask?

(3) Be willing to get in touch with the deep thirst for God which resides at the core of your being.

(4) Learn how to face and handle any doubts that may arise in your heart.

(5) Recognize the subtle nature of sin.

(6) Understand the nature of disappointment and how it hinders your pursuit of God.

(7) Ask God to rid your heart of all fear.

Attend to any of these suggestions, and your spiritual life will move into a new dimension. Attend to all of them and you are destined for the heights.

One word of caution, however—don't try to do too much

all at once. Work on one suggestion at a time. Growth in Christ is not about arriving but moving upward in a godly direction.

And catch again this dominant thought: "Out of the heart spring the issues of life." For when the lips and the heart are in alignment, when they track together with the same, absolute certainty that the rear feet of the deer track with its front feet, then nothing is impossible, whether it be the climbing of mountains or the casting of mountains into the sea.

PRAYER

Father, what can I say? I have heard Your call and I can never be the same again. I ask once more—make this experience a time of rich and joyous discovery. Help me climb higher than I have ever gone before. In Jesus' name. Amen.

FURTHER STUDY

1 Cor. 2; Rom. 8:6; Phil. 2:5; Eph. 4:23
What does the Spirit reveal to us?
What has the Spirit revealed to you?

OTHER BOOKS IN THIS SERIES

If you've enjoyed your experience with this devotional book, look for more Every Day with Jesus® titles by Selwyn Hughes.

Every Day with Jesus: The Lord's Prayer
0-8054-2735-X

Every Day with Jesus: The Spirit-Filled Life
0-8054-2736-8

Every Day with Jesus: The Character of God
0-8054-2737-6

Every Day with Jesus: Hinds' Feet, High Places
0-8054-3088-I

Available July 2004
Every Day with Jesus: The Armor of God
0-8054-3079-2

Available July 2004
Every Day with Jesus: Staying Spiritually Fresh
0-8054-3080-6

ALSO BY SELWYN HUGHES

Every Day Light   0-8054-0188-1
with paintings by Thomas Kinkade

Every Day Light: Water for the Soul   0-8054-1774-5
with paintings by Thomas Kinkade

Every Day Light: Light for the Path   0-8054-2143-2
with paintings by Larry Dyke

Every Day Light: Treasure for the Heart   0-8054-2428-8
with paintings by Larry Dyke

Every Day Light Devotional Journal   0-8054-3309-0

Christ Empowered Living   0-8054-2450-4

Cover to Cover   0-8054-2144-0
A Chronological Plan to Read the Bible in One Year

Hope Eternal   0-8054-1767-2

Jesus-The Light of the World   0-8054-2089-4
with paintings by Larry Dyke

The Selwyn Hughes Signature Series
Born to Praise   0-8054-2091-6
Discovering Life's Greatest Purpose   0-8054-2323-0
God: The Enough   0-8054-2372-9
Prayer: The Greatest Power   0-8054-2349-4

Trusted
All Over the World

Daily Devotionals

Books and Videos

Day and Residential Courses

Counselling Training

Biblical Study Courses

Regional Seminars

Ministry to Women

CWR have been providing training and resources for Christians since the 1960s. From our headquarters at Waverley Abbey House we have been serving God's people with a vision help apply God's Word to everyday life and relationships. The daily devotional *Every Day with Jesus* is read by over three-quarters of a million people in more than 150 countries, and our unique courses in biblical studies an pastoral care are respected all over the world.

For a free brochure about our seminars and cour or a catalogue of CWR resources please contact at the following address:

CWR,
Waverley Abbey House,
Waverley Lane,
Farnham,
Surrey GU9 8EP

Telephone: 01252 784700
Email: mail@cwr.org.uk
Website: www.cwr.org.uk